Macrobiotic Dessert Book

Macrobiotic Dessert Book

Anneliese Wollner

Translated by Gabriele Kushi

Japan Publications, Inc.

Original edition published by Verlag Ost-West Bund, Rehlingen, West Germany in 1986.

Published by JAPAN PUBLICATIONS, INC., Tokyo and New York

Distributors:
UNITED STATES: *Kodansha International/USA, Ltd., through Harper & Row, Publishers, Inc., 10 East 53rd Street, New York, New York 10022.* SOUTH AMERICA: *Harper & Row, Publishers, Inc., International Department.* CANADA: *Fitzhenry & Whiteside Ltd., 195 Allstate Parkway, Markham, Ontario, L3R 4T8.* MEXICO AND CENTRAL AMERICA: *HARLA S. A. de C. V., Apartado 30–546, Mexico 4, D. F.* BRITISH ISLES: *Premier Book Marketing Ltd., 1 Gower Street, London WC1E 6HA.* EUROPEAN CONTINENT: *European Book Service PBD. Strijkviertel 63, 3454 PK de Meern, The Netherlands.* AUSTRALIA AND NEW ZEALAND: *Bookwise International, 1 Jeanes Street, Beverley, South Australia 5007.* THE FAR EAST AND JAPAN: *Japan Publications Trading Co., Ltd., 1–2–1, Sarugaku-cho, Chiyoda-ku, Tokyo 101.*

First edition: August 1988

LCCC No. 87–82909
ISBN 0–87040–700–7

Printed in U.S.A.

Contents

Foreword

The word *macrobiotic* literally means "big life," from the Greek, *macros* or "large," and *bios*, or "life." As the name implies, macrobiotics is concerned with far more than just food and nourishment. It involves a harmonization of opposites and polarities in all aspects of life.

There are a large number of macrobiotic cookbooks available, and an equally impressive number of natural-food dessert books on the market. However, the former may often be limited in variety, and the latter often compromise quality for appearance and are thus not very good for our health and well-being. This book provides a harmony between the two. Nearly all the recipes are based on traditional specialties from around the world, but with the inclusion, when necessary, of more wholesome ingredients. Modification of recipes has been guided by the harmonizing spirit of the principles of macrobiotics.

Generally, a complete macrobiotic meal consists of:
1) Whole cereal grains, unrefined and, if possible, organically grown.
2) *Miso* soup, with beans, sea vegetables, vegetables or mushrooms such as *shiitake* (a Japanese variety). Eaten daily, miso soup is invaluable for our health and well-being. For a change, one could have a *kombu* broth seasoned with *tamari* soy sauce or *shoyu*.
3) Vegetables are chosen according to the seasons and the unique circumstances of each individual. For example, light, leafy green vegetables are more desirable for those engaged in office-type work, or who live in a hot climate, while root vegetables would be taken in smaller proportions by such people.
4) Beans, sea vegetables, and pickled vegetables, beverages, and if desired, small amounts of seafood round out a typical macrobiotic meal.

5) Now, we come to the part of the meal to which we dedicate this book: the *desserts*.

Desserts play more than an unimportant role in our lives. One can think of them as the dot that makes the letter "i" complete. For example, a person's sweet tooth can tell us a lot about his or her condition. For some people, desserts are the main course in their diets, while for others, they are not eaten at all. These are the extremes that all of us confront in our daily lives.

Desserts are not always necessary. Yet, sometimes, they can be an effective medicine. Because desserts can have an expanding, relaxing, and cooling effect, they may be useful when we are tense, cramped, or overtaxed—always remembering the common-sense dictum, "everything in moderation." The dessert proportion should not be more than one-fifth of the whole meal; this includes flour products such as biscuits and pastries, since these generally would not contribute greatly to a wholesome meal.

Desserts consist in principal part of flour, nuts, seeds, and fruits. (Of course, commercial desserts also often contain butter, eggs, and sugar.) Fruit, in comparison to grains and vegetables, is much sweeter or more sour in taste. Excessive consumption of fruits can make our mouths sore. Citrus and other tropical fruits—bananas, mangos, kiwi, and so on—should be avoided by those of us who live in temperate climates; or at least, they should seldom be eaten, and only on very hot days.

Nuts and seeds are not that sweet, but their attraction—and their disadvantage—lies in their high fat content. In addition, it is quite difficult to find nuts that have been organically grown. With all these foods, it is most desirable to look for products that have been grown organically. Many agricultural products are sprayed with pesticides or fungicides such as methylbromide, and they may even be irradiated.

Common errors in macrobiotics often result from the use of flour and its products. Except for whole-flour noodles (without eggs), all other flour products can be considered to have a dessert quality or "snack" character, and thus are considered to be foods eaten only on occasion or in small quantity; this holds true even if they are made into delicious foods such as sandwiches,

9

hors d'oeuvres or pizza! The grinding of grain to make flour creates a different energy from that in the whole grain, even if the flour is a whole-grain flour. Simply, flour is biologically dead, whereas a whole grain still retains its lifeforce.

Let us take desserts simply for what they are: palatable delicacies for "after table" occasions that make our days more enjoyable, or as delicious food that raises our festive spirits during holidays. With this in mind, I wish all food connoisseurs and gourmets much fun as they explore this cookbook, and I hope that the recipes will bring joy to your kitchen.

FRED WOLLNER

Preface

A life in harmony with nature: Many wish for it, some reach it. It takes a lot of effort, still it is so simple.

One path to this goal is to change your ingrained eating habits. Eat what was prepared with love, according to the laws of nature, and with that you will help your body and soul. Nourishment and love sustain our daily lives. Use these keys of knowledge and intuition, and many doors will be opened for you.

My special gratitude goes to Zeane and MayLi, my leaders on this journey to a harmonious life. In addition, my thanks go to Mumi Krupica, whose practical instruction has been a great help to me and to many others.

> One lifetime is filled
> with not even a hundred years
> but is always filled
> with a thousand years of sorrow.
> The noontime is short
> And bitter long is the night.
> Why not reach for the light,
> look for the brief pleasures
> for yourself, when, if not today?
> What are you waiting for
> year after year?
> — Chinese Wisdom.

Introduction

With this book, I want to show readers that it is possible to prepare great-tasting bakery goods and desserts without the use of chemical baking aids, or without eggs, dairy food, or refined sugar!

Instead of chemical baking aids, only vegetable margarines and oils are used in the recipes. When fluffed up in a natural way, these oils release steam during baking, which then raises the dough. Biological leavening agents include yeast and sourdough. However, yeast puts a strain on the intestines, and so in some cake recipes, sourdough is used instead, even though sourdough is usually only used to bake bread.

In the recipes contained in this book, eggs are not necessary. You will not miss them, particularly if you keep in mind that a chicken egg will contain 100 to 200 million bacteria after only a few days. These bacteria cause the deterioration of the egg so that it will become rotten; these bacteria will also enter the digestive tract if you eat these same eggs.

Cow's milk is not nearly so healthy as one might be led to believe. First, it is pasteurized, which kills the lactobacillus that aids in digestion. Secondly, preservatives are often added to the milk. However, the most important problem with milk is that it is nourishment intended for the development of baby cows, not for the nourishment of adult (or baby) humans.

Instead of cow's milk in our desserts or elsewhere in our diet, there is a very tasty "substitute" in soymilk. It contains a lot of protein, and is made from the soybean. If you do purchase and use soymilk, make certain that it is not sweetened with sugar.

Instead of white, refined sugar, sweeteners used in the recipes include maple syrup, grain sweeteners made from rice or barley, or unsulfured dried fruits. Brown sugar or raw turbinado sugar are not used in the recipes because they are refined sugars as well. These sugars deplete vitamin-B stores just as much as common white sugar. Marmalade is often mentioned in the recipes; you can make it yourself, or buy varieties without sugar in natural food stores.

Nearly all recipes contain a touch of sea salt. A little salt brings out the sweetness in foods, while at the same time providing a balance from excess sweeteners and fruits. Instead of regular table salt, it is far better to use sea salt since it contains important trace minerals such as iodine, bromine, copper, and others.

The recipes consist fully of whole grain flour. Refined flour often contains little if any germ or fiber; the former provides important nutrients, while the latter is an important aid to digestion. Therefore, whole-grain flours contain B vitamins and vitamin E, and trace minerals such as iron, copper, and zinc.

This book should be a source to inspire you to use your own imagination. Everyone has one's own personal style and manner, in the kitchen and elsewhere. The recipes can be thought of simply as guidelines to let your culinary imagination run free, rather than as rigid rules to follow strictly.

Finally, I wish you much fun with trying out these recipes, and most of all that they will all turn out well!

The Classical Doughs

In the following section, you will find five main doughs, which you adapt in whatever way you choose for your recipes. Accompanying each recipe are additional directions and pointers concerning the doughs.

Shortcake Dough

1 lb. whole wheat flour
1/2 lb. vegetable margarine
2 tsps. barley malt or rice syrup
1/2 cup cold water
Natural vanilla
Touch of sea salt
Grated lemon rind

The whole wheat flour, margarine, and water should be cold if possible. You can put the ingredients in the refrigerator for 1 hour prior to mixing them together.

Combine all ingredients and knead them thoroughly. Then, place the dough in a cool place for 30 minutes before using it.

Puff Pastry

1 lb. whole wheat pastry flour
1 lb. vegetable margarine
1 cup water
Touch of sea salt

Mix the margarine with ¼ of the flour, form a flat brick from the mixture, and place it in the refrigerator. Next, work the leftover ingredients into a smooth dough. Then, fold it into a wet towel, and place it in the refrigerator for 30 minutes.

After this dough has cooled, roll it out flat and roll the margarine brick onto the dough. Bang the brick flat, sprinkle some flour over it, and roll it out carefully. Fold the dough in thirds, then place it in the refrigerator for 30 minutes.

Sprinkle flour on the dough, roll it out again, then fold it in fourths. Let it cool for another 30 minutes.

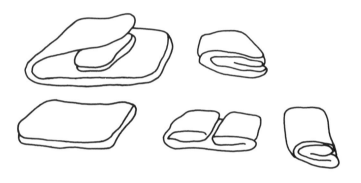

Strudel Dough

1 lb. whole wheat pastry flour
5 tsps. sunflower oil
1 cup water
Touch of sea salt

Mix all ingredients together and knead to a smooth dough. Continue kneading for an additional 20 minutes and then form the dough into a ball. Cover the ball with oil, and let it sit in a covered bowl in a warm place for 1 hour.

Choux (Fire) Pastry Dough

1/3 lb. whole wheat pastry flour
6 Tbsps. vegetable margarine
1 cup water
Touch of sea salt

Combine the water, margarine, and sea salt and bring to a boil.
Mix in the whole wheat flour. On a low heat, continue to stir
until the dough that is formed is loosened from the bottom of
the pot. Put the dough in a bowl and let it cool.

Sourdough

This dough is used in place of yeasted dough, because it is
easier to digest.

Starter: 5 tsps. fine rye flour
Water
Barley malt

Combine all ingredients and mix into a thin dough. Cover and let
sit for 3 days.

Dough: 2 lbs. whole wheat flour
1/2 lb. vegetable margarine
2 cups warm water
Touch of sea salt
Grated lemon rind
1 tsp. sourdough starter

Mix ingredients, plus the starter, into a smooth dough, then
cover and let stand for 3 hours in a warm place.

1. Pies and Tarts

Apple-Orange Cake

Tofu gives this fruitcake a very light and flaky crust.

1/3 lb. whole wheat flour
1/4 lb. *tofu*
3 1/2 oz. vegetable margarine
1 cup rice syrup
Touch of sea salt
1 cup coarse whole meal crumbs
2 apples
2 oranges
1/2 cup apricot marmalade (unsweetened, no added sugar)

Put the flour in a baking tin. Make a depression in the middle, and place the margarine, rice syrup, and sea salt in it. Press the *tofu* with your hands to remove excess water, and add it. Knead the dough well and wrap it in a damp towel. Leave the dough overnight in the refrigerator.

Roll out the dough in a thin layer on a dampened baking tray, then sprinkle it with the coarse whole meal crumbs. Lay the peeled and sliced apples and oranges on top. If you desire, you can cover the dough with apricot marmalade before topping it off with the apples and oranges.

Bake at 220°C. (425°F.) for 45 to 50 minutes.

Baklava

Puff Pastry (see recipe)
Filling: 1/2 lb. walnuts
1/2 cup rice syrup
Natural vanilla
Frosting: 1 cup water
Juice of 3 lemons
1/2 cup rice syrup

Cover an oven-proof baking dish with tin foil. Make alternate layers of the puff pastry and filling, starting with the puff pastry. The last layer should also be puff pastry dough. Cut the whole into pieces of about 1½ by 2½ inches, then pour the frosting over all of it.

Bake at 220°C. (425°F.) for 40 minutes.

Rhubarb-Rice Cake

Instead of flour, whole grains are used in this cake.

1 lb. brown rice
1 qt. water
3 1/2 Tbsps. grated coconut
1 cup raisins
1/2 cup *amazake*
Clove powder
Cinnamon
Touch of sea salt
1 1/2 lbs. fresh rhubarb

Wash the brown rice and cook for 40 minutes. Meanwhile, peel the rhubarb and cut it into small pieces. Mix these pieces with the cooked rice and other ingredients, and put on a baking tray. Sprinkle with grated coconut.
Bake at 210°C. (410°F.) for 1 hour.

Apple Pie With Grid Crust

You can vary the filling of this pie made from shortcake dough. Instead of apples, you might want to use cherries, pears, apricots, and so on.

Shortcake dough (see recipe)
Filling: **2 lbs. apples, finely sliced**
1/2 cup raisins
Touch of sea salt
Cinnamon

Roll out the shortcake dough about ¼-inch thick, and place 2/3 of it on the bottom of a pie tin. Combine the filling, and add to the pie crust. Cut the leftover dough into small strips, and arrange it as a grid over the filling.
Bake at 210°C. (410°F.) for 1 hour.

Fruitbread

This is a recipe for one of the most traditional pastries of the Christmas holidays. However, it is not just for the end of the year!

2 lbs. whole wheat flour
2 cups warm water
Touch of sea salt
4 oz. raisins
4 oz. sliced almonds
4 oz. chopped hazelnuts
8 oz. dried prunes
8 oz. dried pears
1 tsp. cinnamon
1 tsp. natural vanilla
Grated lemon rind
1 tsp. sourdough starter (see recipe)

Soak the fruit for 2 hours and then cook for 15 minutes in the soaking water. Cut the fruit into pieces and mix thoroughly with the other ingredients. Knead the resulting dough for 10 minutes and put it in a baking tin which has been laid out with sliced almonds. Cover the dough and let it rest for 12 hours.
Bake at 200°C. (395°F.) for 1 hour.

Austrian Apple Strudel

This is a typical Austrian specialty, and tastes good with warm vanilla sauce (see *Vanilla Sauce* recipe).

Strudel dough (see recipe)
Filling: 2 lbs. apples
1/2 lb. raisins
1/2 lb. whole grain crumbs
Cinnamon

Prepare a strudel dough. While the dough is resting, cut the apples into very fine slices. After the dough has sat for 1 hour, roll it out on a cotton towel that has been covered with flour. Continue to stretch the dough into a thin layer by pulling it with your hands.

Cover the dough with the finely sliced apples and raisins. Toast the crumbs in some oil, and together with the cinnamon, sprinkle over the apples and raisins. With the help of the cotton towel, roll the dough together.

Place on a baking tin and bake at 210°C. (410°F.) for 40 minutes.

Cherry Strudel

Strudel dough (see below)
***Filling:* 2 lbs. pitted cherries**
Touch of sea salt
1 cup whole wheat semolina

Prepare a strudel dough, following the instructions for the Austrian Apple Strudel (see previous recipe). However, for filling, add cherries and steamed semolina over the flour instead of using the Austrian Apple Strudel filling.

To prepare the semolina, dry-roast it, then pour it into ½ cup boiling salted water while stirring constantly. Let it simmer on a low flame for 15 minutes. It is then ready to be combined with the cherries to be used as filling for this strudel.

Tofu Strudel

This strudel recipe, with a *tofu* filling, is derived from a popular cheese strudel. Served with hot vanilla sauce, *tofu* strudel is like a traditional Austrian *millirahmstrudel*.

Prepare a strudel dough as in the Apple Strudel recipe. For the filling use the following ingredients:

Filling: **14 oz. *tofu***
Natural vanilla
Grated lemon rind
6 Tbsps. rice syrup
1/2 cup raisins
1 Tbsp. miso

To prepare the filling, mix the *tofu*, natural vanilla, lemon rind, and rice syrup in a blender with a little water. After it has become smooth, mix the raisins and *miso* into the blended *tofu*. Add to the strudel.

Apple-Poppy Seed Strudel

This delicious Hungarian specialty comes from Mrs. Mumi Krupica in Austria, where she is known for her artistic wholegrain baking. The preparation is the same as with the Apple Strudel. The filling for the strudel consists of 1 pound of finely sliced apples and the following poppy seed filling:

Poppy Seed Filling: **1 lb. poppy seeds**
2 cups rice syrup
Natural vanilla
Grated lemon rind
1/2 cup washed raisins
1/2 qt. water

Add the raisins, rice syrup, natural vanilla and lemon rind to the water, and bring to a boil. Mix in the poppy seeds, and let simmer on a low flame for 15 minutes. Bake for 40 minutes at 210°C. (410°F.).

Poppy Seed Cake

Shape the shortcake dough so that it is ½-inch thick on a baking tray, and bake until it is light brown at 210°C. (410°F.). Cover with the poppy seed filling (given in the previous recipe), and sprinkle with sliced almonds. Bake an additional 15 minutes, and cut into pieces.

Crumb Cake

Prepare a dough following the sourdough recipe. Place the dough in a baking tray, cover it with halved apricots, and sprinkle with crumbs.

Crumbs: Mix 10 ounces of whole wheat flour with 7 ounces of cold margarine. Add some cinnamon and natural vanilla, and 3 tablespoons of rice syrup. This mixture will fall into crumbs.

Bake the cake at 180° to 200°C. (about 375°F.) for 50 minutes.

Sacher Torte

With this torte, you can bring the magic of a real Vienna coffee-house into your home.

> 1 lb. bulgur, ground into semolina
> 1/2 lb. grated hazelnuts
> 14 oz. *tofu*
> 1/2 cup rice syrup
> 1 cup carob powder
> Natural vanilla
> Touch of sea salt
> Grated orange rind

Mix the bulgur semolina with the hazelnuts, natural vanilla, sea salt, orange rind, and carob powder. Mix the *tofu* and rice syrup together in a blender. Mix the dry and wet mixtures together, and let sit for 10 minutes. Put this mixture into an oiled cake pan, and bake at 200°C. (395°F.) for 1 hour. Coat with carob cream (see recipe). —See page 53.

Malakoff Torte

This torte is prepared very quickly and does not need to be baked.

> 2 packages unsweetened whole grain zwieback
> crackers (rusks)
> 1 cup instant grain coffee
> 1/2 cup hazelnut butter
> 1/2 cup arrowroot
> 3 Tbsps. agar flakes
> 1 cup barley malt or rice syrup
> Grated lemon rind
> Natural vanilla
> Touch of sea salt

Dissolve the grain coffee in 1 quart of warm water. Place the crackers in a baking pan and pour the coffee over them.

Combine the hazelnut butter, grain syrup, agar, lemon rind, vanilla, and salt with ½ quart of water, and bring to a boil.

Dissolve the arrowroot in some cold water and mix it into the boiling mixture while stirring constantly. Simmer for 10 minutes on a low flame until it thickens.

Let this cream cool sufficiently to add to the crackers, then place alternating layers of crackers and cream in the pan. When the cream has cooled completely, the torte can be cut.

Strawberry Torte

With this torte, other fruit can be substituted for the strawberries.

Prepare a shortcake dough, including an additional 3½ ounces of grated hazelnuts. Place the dough in an oiled fruit-torte pan, and bake at 200°C. (395°F.) until golden brown. Turn the torte upside down and cover with strawberry marmalade and halved strawberries. Cover with an agar gelatin (see below).

Agar Gelatin: Bring ½ quart of water mixed with ¼ package of agar flakes to a boil. Simmer for 10 minutes, then sweeten with 3 tablespoons of rice syrup and let cool.

When the agar gelatin is lukewarm, pour it over the strawberries. When the gelatin becomes cold, it will solidify.

It is preferable to use agar flakes or bars. Agar in powder form is usually made by precipitation with potassium chloride and is bleached chemically. —See page 52.

Linzer Torte

The Linzer Torte is a very famous spice cake from Austria.

2 lbs. whole wheat flour
1 lb. vegetable margarine
1 lb. grated almonds
Grated lemon rind
Cinnamon
Natural vanilla
1 Tbsp. *miso*
10 oz. barley malt or rice syrup
1/2 cup unsweetened currant marmalade (black or red)
2 Tbsps. *mirin*
Cloves

Combine all the ingredients except the marmalade into a smooth dough, then let rest for 30 minutes. Roll out ⅔ of the dough, place it in an oiled pie tin, then cover with the marmalade. Roll out the leftover dough, and cut into fine strips. Lay these strips in a grid on top of the marmalade. Spread some rice syrup on the grid as a glaze.
Bake at 180°C. (360°F.) for 1 hour.

Tofu Torte

A light and refreshing summer torte, made from shortcake dough.

Shortcake dough (see recipe)
1 lb. *tofu*
1/2 cup rice syrup
3 1/2 oz. dried apricots
Natural vanilla
Grated lemon rind

Roll out the shortcake dough in a thin layer on an oiled cake pan. Cook the dried apricots for 15 minutes and mix them with the remaining ingredients in a blender. Cover the torte base with this mixture.
Bake at 120° to 200°C. (275° to 395°F.) for 50 minutes.

Torte Decoration

This is a recipe for a cream which can be used with a pastry bag for decorating cakes and tortes.

1 cup soymilk
2 Tbsps. agar flakes
3 Tbsps. almond butter
3 Tbsps. arrowroot flour
1 Tbsp. rice syrup

Bring the soymilk, rice syrup, and almond butter to a boil. Dissolve the arrowroot in cold water. Add the agar and dissolved arrowroot to the boiling soymilk and almond butter. Let this mixture cool until it is lukewarm, then use it. If it cools too much, it will become too hard to use with a pastry bag.

2. Cookies and Biscuits

Mocha Eclair

This French dessert is also called a "love bone."
 Prepare a choux pastry dough, and with a pastry bag, squirt 3-inch-long strips of the dough onto an oiled baking tin. Bake at 210°C. (410°F.) for 20 minutes. When it is still warm, cut away the cover and fill with:

Mocha Filling: **2 cups soymilk**
5 Tbsps. cornstarch
5 Tbsps. instant grain coffee
5 Tbsps. rice syrup
Natural vanilla
Touch of sea salt

Combine the soymilk, grain coffee, rice syrup, natural vanilla, and sea salt, and bring to a boil. Mix in the corn starch, and simmer for 10 minutes. Let the cream cool so that it can thicken.
 After adding the filling to the eclairs, place the covers back on and serve.

Almond Cream Puff

Prepare a choux pastry dough, and using a pastry bag, place small balls of pastry on a baking pan. Bake at 210°C. (410°F.) for 12 to 15 minutes. Cut these open while they are still warm, and fill them with the following cream:

Almond Cream: 2 cups soymilk
5 Tbsps. cornstarch
5 Tbsps. almond butter
5 Tbsps. rice syrup
Natural vanilla
Touch of sea salt

Bring the soymilk, almond butter, rice syrup, natural vanilla, and sea salt to a boil. Stir in the cornstarch and let simmer for 10 minutes. Let the almond cream cool.

Be sure to put the covers to the cream puffs back on after you have added the almond cream filling.

Florentine

This nut specialty has its origins in Florence, but it is well-known beyond Italy.

1 cup soymilk
3 Tbsps. rice syrup
7 oz. slivered almonds
1 1/2 oz. homemade *aranzini* (see recipe)
2 oz. whole wheat flour

2 oz. margarine
5 1/2 oz. halved almonds
Natural vanilla
Cinnamon
Carob cream (see recipe)

Bring the soymilk and margarine to a boil. Stir the slivered almonds, *aranzini*, rice syrup, vanilla, cinnamon, and flour into the hot milk and let simmer for several minutes. After it has cooled somewhat, put small balls of the mixture onto an aluminum-foil-covered baking pan. Add the halved almonds on top of these balls.

Bake at 210°C. (410°F.) for 45 minutes.

Remove the baked florentines immediately from the baking pan, and cover their bottoms with carob cream.

Hussar Doughnut

Prepare shortcake dough, adding 7 ounces of roasted hazelnuts to the dough. Form the dough into small balls on an oiled baking pan. Make a depression in the middle of each ball.

Bake at 210°C. (410°F.) for 25 minutes.

While the doughnuts are still hot, fill each hollow with strawberry marmalade.

Linzer Pastry Wheel

Prepare shortcake dough, roll it out, and cut out round cookies from the dough. Every other cookie should have three holes.

Bake at 210°C. (410° F.) for 25 minutes and let cool.

Cover the whole cookies with strawberry marmalade, and cover these with the cookies with holes, "sandwich" style. Instead of sprinkling these cookies with powdered sugar, you can use flour of *kinako* (roasted soy flour).

Viennese Vanilla Crescents

Prepare a shortcake dough with ½ pound of grated almonds and 3½ ounces of wheat germ. Form the dough into pencil-thick rolls, and cut into 2-inch-long pieces. Bend these lengths into a crescent shape and bake at 210°C. (410°F.). When they are still hot, cover the crescents with rice syrup and roll in the grated almonds.

Garibaldi

Prepare puff pastry dough, then roll it out into two equal halves. Spread rice syrup over one of the halves, then cover the surface with raisins. Now place the other pastry dough half on top. Cut this into rectangles, and place on a baking pan.
Bake at 230°C. (445°F.) for 25 minutes.

Marmalade Croissant

Prepare puff pastry dough for this crunchy croissant, and roll it out into large 3-inch squares. Fill these squares with un-sweetened marmalade, then fold them together to form the croissant.
Bake to a golden brown at 230°C. (445°F.). —See page 52.

Nut Croissant

Roll out the shortcake dough into 3-inch squares, and cover each with the following filling:

Nut Filling: 1/2 lb. grated walnuts
1/2 cup rice syrup
Grated lemon rind
5 Tbsps. raisins
Natural vanilla

Bring all the ingredients except the nuts to a boil in 1 cup of water. Stir in the nuts, and simmer for 15 minutes.

After adding the nut filling, fold the square and form a croissant.

Bake at 210°C. (410°F.) for 25 minutes.

Tofu Squares

Roll out the puff pastry dough, and cut into squares. Place 1 tablespoon of *tofu* filling (see *Tofu Strudel* recipe) in the middle of each. Fold the four corners in, and place a flower, shaped from dough, in the middle where the four corners meet. Bake briefly at 230°C. (445°F.).

Apple Pyramids

This is a biscuit made of puff pastry dough.

Puff pastry dough (see recipe)
Filling: **2 lbs. apples**
1 cup raisins
Cinnamon

Wash the apples, cut into fine slices, and mix with raisins and cinnamon. Roll out the puff pastry dough into squares and put some filling on the center of each square. Fold the corners of the squares in, squeezing the ends with a fork. Bake to a golden brown at 230°C. (445°F.).

Carob-Filled Walnut Cookies

Prepare a shortcake dough, adding 3½ ounces of grated walnuts. Roll out the dough, then cut it into round cookies. Bake the cookies at 210°C. (410°F.) until golden brown. Use a slightly thick carob cream (see recipe) as the filling between two cookies, creating a cookie "sandwich." Glaze the top of the cookies with maple syrup.

Little Bethmann Biscuits

These biscuits take their name from the Bethmann family of Frankfurt, who created these biscuits around 1830.

1 jar almond butter
1/2 cup rice syrup
2 1/2 oz. blanched, halved almonds
2 oz. cornstarch

Heat the almond butter with the rice syrup, and stir in the cornstarch until it thickens. Cool the mixture and form small balls, placing them on a lightly oiled baking tin. Place 3 almond halves on each.

Bake at 210°C. (410°F.) to a golden brown. —See page 55.

Black And White Cookies

1 lb. whole grain flour
1/2 lb. vegetable margarine
1/2 cup rice syrup
1 cup carob powder
1/2 cup instant grain coffee

Whip the margarine, and add it to the flour, along with the rice syrup and enough water to form a smooth dough. Split the dough in half, and to one half add the grain coffee and carob powder. Let the doughs cool for 1 hour.

After cooling, put the light dough on top of the dark, and roll together. Again, cool the dough for 1 hour.

Cut the dough into thin slices and bake at 210° to 230°C. (410° to 445°F.) for 20 minutes.

Almond Triangles

Instead of using almonds, you can substitute pine nuts, chopped walnuts, or other nuts in this recipe.

5 cups fine oat flakes
1/2 lb. slivered almonds
1/4 lb. vegetable margarine
Natural vanilla
Cinnamon
Almonds cut into sticks for sprinkling
5 Tbsps. barley malt or rice syrup

Mix the oat flakes with the margarine. Add the other ingredients except the almond sticks, and knead to a dough. Place the dough on an oiled baking pan, and roll it out. Cover with maple syrup and sprinkle with the almond sticks. Bake at 210°C. (410°F.) for 30 minutes.
After it cools, cut into triangles.

Nani's Cookies

4 cups fine oat flakes
Touch of sea salt
Grated orange rind
2 cups grated hazelnuts
2 Tbsps. vegetable margarine
5 Tbsps. rice syrup
Natural vanilla
Whole hazelnuts for decoration

Mix all ingredients (except the whole hazelnuts) with enough warm water to knead into a soft dough. Take small pieces from the dough and form balls. Place these balls on an oiled baking pan, and decorate each with a whole hazelnut.
Bake until golden brown at 210°C. (410°F.).

Northern Spice Flowers

3 1/2 oz. vegetable margarine
5 1/2 oz. rice syrup
1/2 lb. whole wheat flour
1/2 tsp. grated ginger
1/2 tsp. cinnamon
1/2 tsp. gingerbread spice
Touch of sea salt

Stir the margarine until creamy. Mix flour and spices together with the rice syrup, and add to the margarine. Cool this dough for 1 to 2 hours, then roll it out into a thin sheet. Cut the dough into round cookies about 2 inches in diameter, and flower-shaped cookies about 1¼ inches in diameter.
Bake at 210°C. (410°F.) for 30 minutes.

After baking, form a sandwich with one round cookie and one flower-shaped cookie, with unsweetened marmalade as the filling. —See page 50.

Leckerli (Tidbits)

7 oz. vegetable margarine
5 Tbsps. rice syrup
6 Tbsps. carob powder
Natural vanilla
14 Tbsps. whole wheat flour

Whip the margarine with a whisk until frothy. Slowly stir in the remaining ingredients. Put in a pastry bag, and on an oiled baking pan, form small wavy stripes.
Bake at 210°C. (410°F.) for 20 minutes.

Coconut Kisses

This biscuit is also known as a "coconut macaroon."

4 oz. vegetable margarine
4 oz. coconut flakes
4 1/2 oz. whole wheat flour
1/2 cup barley malt

Stir the margarine until it is cream-like, then add the flour and coconut flakes. After these have been well-mixed, add the barley malt. Form into small balls and place on an oiled baking pan. Bake at 210°C. (410°F.) for 25 minutes.

Kokoh Cookies

1 cup *kokoh* (see recipe)
1 cup whole wheat flour
4 Tbsps. sunflower oil
Touch of sea salt
5 Tbsps. rice syrup

Mix all the ingredients together with as much water as is needed to form an elastic dough. Roll the dough out, and cut into various shapes.
Bake at 210°C. (410°F.) for 15 to 20 minutes.

Buckwheat Pretzels

These pretzels are for nibbling, and can be stored for a long time.

5 1/2 oz. buckwheat flour
3 1/2 oz. whole wheat flour
4 oz. grated almonds
3 oz. vegetable margarine
6 Tbsps. rice syrup
Touch of sea salt

Mix the flours, almonds, sea salt, and rice syrup together. Melt the margarine, and add it and some cold water, and knead to form a dough. With hands covered with flour, form the dough into pretzels and put on a baking pan. Bake at 210°C. (410°F.) for 25 minutes.

Cinnamon Stars

1/2 lb. fine oat flakes
2 oz. grated almonds
5 1/2 oz. vegetable margarine
1 tsp. cinnamon
Touch of sea salt
Grated lemon rind
5 Tbsps. rice syrup
3 1/2 oz. fine whole wheat flour

Lightly toast the oat flakes in a pan. Combine all the ingredients and knead into a dough, adding water as necessary. Cool for 2 hours in a refrigerator. Roll the dough into a thin layer, and cut into stars.
Bake at 230°C. (445°F.) for 15 minutes.

Sweet Gingerbread

2 lbs. whole wheat flour
1 lb. vegetable margarine
16 oz. barley malt or rice syrup
2 Tbsps. rose water
2–3 Tbsps. gingerbread spice
1 Tbsp. miso
Grated orange rind
10 oz. roasted and grated almonds
5 1/2 oz. chopped walnuts

Heat the grain syrup and margarine until the mixture becomes a liquid. Let it cool, and then mix all the ingredients into a firm dough. Wrap the dough with a towel, and put it in a cool place for one day.

Roll out the dough and place on an oiled baking pan. Bake at 175°C. (350°F.) for 25 minutes.

While the gingerbread is still warm, cut it into pieces, glaze with barley malt, and decorate with peeled almonds.

42

Gingerbread Man

In the United States, gingerbread men are used as ornaments to decorate Christmas trees.

1 cup whole wheat flour
4 Tbsps. rice syrup
1 level tsp. finely grated ginger
5 Tbsps. water

Mix all ingredients together well, and knead into a smooth dough. Roll the dough out and form little men out of it. Place the men on a baking pan.
Bake at 210°C. (410°F.) for 25 minutes.

Buckwheat Sticks

These biscuits, which come from Japan, are not baked, but deep-fried.

1 cup whole wheat flour
1/2 cup buckwheat flour
Touch of sea salt
1 Tbsp. sesame oil
1/2 cup water
Sunflower oil for deep-frying

Mix all ingredients together well, roll out the dough, and cut into strips 1¼-inches wide. Cut these strips width-wise into ⅛-inch-wide strips. Heat the sunflower oil, and deep-fry the sticks. Soak up excess oil on a paper towel.

Chinese Date Sandwich Cookies

These sandwich cookies make delicious Christmas treats.

1/2 lb. whole wheat flour
1 cup rice syrup
3 1/2 oz. chopped walnuts
5 1/2 oz. seedless dates, finely chopped
Touch of sea salt

Mix all ingredients together well; if more liquid is needed to form a dough, use soymilk. Roll out the dough to a ½-inch thickness, and put on an oiled baking pan. Bake at 230°C. (445°F.) for 30 minutes.

After baking and while it is still warm, cut into rectangles, cover with rice syrup, and sprinkle with cinnamon.

Lemon Biscuits

A summertime biscuit recipe.

1/2 lb. corn flour
5 1/2 oz. vegetable margarine
3 Tbsps. lemon juice
Grated lemon rind
Natural vanilla
2 oz. washed raisins
3 Tbsps. rice syrup
Touch of sea salt

Combine the corn flour, vanilla, salt, raisins, and lemon rind, and mix well. Then, add the margarine, lemon juice, and rice syrup, and mix to form a dough. Form small balls from this dough, and place them on an oiled baking pan. Bake at 230°C. (445°F.) for 10 minutes.

Sesame Spirals

These spirals can be a light biscuit for between-meal snacks.
Prepare a puff pastry dough, roll it into a thin layer, and cut into ¾- by 2-inch strips. Hold the ends of each strip and twist into a three-fold spiral. Place these on a baking pan, brush with soy sauce, and sprinkle some sesame seeds on them. Bake at 230°C. (445°F.) for 25 minutes.

Punch Balls

A well-known dessert for New Year's Eve.

**1 pack of whole wheat zwieback (rusk)
crackers, unsweetened
6 Tbsps. apple-pear concentrate
1/2 cup *mirin*
Juice from 1 orange
3 1/2 oz. grated hazelnuts**

Break up the crackers and soak in *mirin* and water until they are soft. Mix and knead well with the other ingredients. Form into balls and roll in chopped nuts. —See page 54.

Bulgarian Hibiscus Biscuits

Prepare a shortcake dough, roll it out, and cut into small rings. Put on an oiled baking pan and bake at 210°C. (410°F.) for 25 minutes.

After baking, and when the biscuits are still hot, make "double ring" sandwiches, filling each with hibiscus marmalade.

Nut Swirls

A biscuit for afternoon coffee or tea.

Prepare a sourdough, then roll it into a large rectangle about ¼-inch thick. Cover with softened margarine. Cover this with 5 ounces of raisins that have been washed and soaked for ten minutes, 2½ ounces of grated almonds, and ½ cup of rice syrup.

Roll up the dough, and cut into ½-inch-thick, round pieces. Let rise on a baking tin for 20 minutes, then bake at 230°C. (445°F.) for 40 minutes.

Black Comets

7 oz. vegetable margarine
10 oz. very fine whole wheat flour
2 oz. carob powder
1/2 cup rice syrup
Touch of sea salt

Stir the margarine to a creamy consistency. Mix the flour with the salt and carob powder, and work it, bit by bit, into the margarine. Place this mixture into a pastry bag, and squirt small roses with tails like a comet on an oiled baking tin.

Bake immediately at 230°C. (445°F.).

3. Hot and Cold Desserts

Rice Pudding

An easy-to-digest pudding made from whole grains.

**1 cup brown rice
2 cups soymilk
1/2 cup washed raisins
2 oz. vegetable margarine
1 cup rice syrup
1 cinnamon stick
1 lemon peel
Touch of sea salt
7 oz. *tofu***

Cook the brown rice together with the soymilk, cinnamon stick, and lemon peel. After the rice has cooked, mix in the margarine, raisins, and rice syrup. Blend the *tofu* into a smooth consistency, then add it to the rice mixture. Take an oiled baking form, and sprinkle whole grain crumbs into it. Fill this form with the rice mixture.
Bake at 250°C. (480°F.) for 30 minutes.

Baked Stakes

This is a traditional Austrian dessert.

5 whole meal graham rolls
1 lb. apples
Grated lemon rind
2 oz. raisins
3 1/2 oz. chopped hazelnuts
1 cup rice syrup
Cinnamon

Cut the graham rolls into slices and put them in a bowl. Pour
the rice syrup, mixed with ½ cup of water, over the slices. Peel
and core the apples, and cut into fine slices. Mix the nuts, lemon
rind, and cinnamon into the roll slices. In an oiled pudding
form, place alternate layers of roll slices, apples and raisins.
Bake at 250°C. (480°F.) for 40 minutes, then divide into serving
portions.

Poppy Seed Noodles

You can even make desserts out of noodles. Try this recipe with
walnuts instead of poppy seeds as well.

1 pack broad whole wheat noodles
1 cup soymilk
5 Tbsps. rice syrup
3 1/2 oz. poppy seeds

Boil the noodles in slightly salted water. Heat the soymilk
together with the rice syrup, and stir in the poppy seeds. After
it has come to a boil, let simmer for about 10 minutes. Mix
this poppy seed filling in with the cooked noodles. Serve warm.

49

Plum-Pudding (See page 75.)

Greek Love Strips (See page 58.)

Maple Candies (See page 99.)

Northern Spice Flowers (See page 38.)

Tofu-Fruit Cream (See page 81.)

Strawberry Torte (See page 27.)

52

Marmalade Croissant
(See page 34.)

Fruit Jelly (See page 84.)

Happy Hedgehogs (See page 60.)

Carob Truffles (See page 89.)

Sacher Torte (See page 26.)

54

Punch Balls (See page 44.)

Nut Kanten (See page 82.)

Sesame Taffy (See page 85.)

Little Bethmann Biscuits (See page 36.)

Stuffed Dates (See page 90.)

Azuki Manju (See page 59.)

Raisin Doughnuts

Prepare a choux pastry dough, and at the end, add 3½ ounces of raisins and 3½ ounces of chopped almonds. With a tablespoon, scoop out pieces of dough, and deep-fry in hot oil so that the doughnuts are swimming. Drain excess oil on a paper towel and serve.

Sweet Mochi

You can buy brown rice *mochi* in many natural food stores. *Mochi* is made from sweet rice, which is pounded to a sticky dough and formed into small blocks. It can keep a long time when dried and wrapped. *Mochi* is a great source of energy for both adults and children, and in Japan, is an essential food for parties and festive occasions.

Cut the *mochi* into ½-inch-thick slices and deep-fry in hot oil; the pieces should puff up slightly and break open. Dissolve 5 tablespoons of barley malt in a bowl of water. Dip the deep-fried *mochi* in the barley malt solution, and roll them in *kinako*.

Tofu Doughnuts

1/2 lb. *tofu*
2 oz. vegetable margarine
4 oz. whole wheat flour
3 Tbsps. rice syrup
Natural vanilla
Cinnamon

Stir the margarine together with the rice syrup, cinnamon, and vanilla until frothy. Add the flour and creamy *tofu* (blend the *tofu* to make it creamy), and mix thoroughly. With a tablespoon, take small pieces and deep-fry in hot oil.

Stork's Nests

This recipe is one way to deliciously dress up apple compote.

10 oz. whole wheat flour
2 Tbsps. rice syrup
1/2 cup soymilk
Touch of sea salt
Natural vanilla

Mix the flour with salt, rice syrup, and vanilla. Add the soy-milk to form a firm dough. Form walnut-sized pieces of dough, and put them on a floured board. Sprinkle these pieces with flour and let rest for 30 minutes.

Roll out the pieces into ¼-inch-wide strips, being careful not to fray the edges of the dough. Lift these strips carefully, and deep-fry in hot oil until they are a light brown. Sprinkle with cinnamon.

Greek Love Strips

Prepare shortcake dough, adding some grated orange rind to the recipe. Roll out the shortcake dough a few millimeters thick (about the thickness of the back of a kitchen knife blade), and cut into ½-inch by 6-inch strips. Tie each strip so that there is a loose knot in each. Deep-fry in hot oil. Cover with rice syrup, and sprinkle with cinnamon and grated walnuts. —See page 49.

Blueberry Pancakes

1 cup whole wheat flour
1 cup fresh blueberries
3 Tbsps. rice malt
Touch of sea salt

Mix all the ingredients with water to form a thick batter, but make it moist enough to flow easily into a hot pan. Oil the pan liberally, since the fruit in the batter makes the cakes stick to the pan. Fry until both sides are golden brown.

Azuki Manju

These dough pockets are a favorite in Japan. They can also be filled with vegetables.

3 cups whole wheat flour
1 cup *amazake*
2 cups puréed *azuki* beans
3 Tbsps. rice syrup
Touch of sea salt
Cinnamon
3 Tbsps. sunflower oil

To prepare puréed *azuki* beans, cook the beans, then purée in a blender. Make a smooth dough out of the flour, salt, oil, and some water. Roll out the dough and cut into circles 2-inches in diameter. Cover one half of these circles with a filling made of puréed *azuki* beans, rice syrup, *amazake*, and cinnamon. Fold the dough over to cover the filling, and press the edges together with a fork.

Cook these little half-moon pastries in a steamer, or cook them in hot water with a pinch of salt. —See page 56.

Coupe Poire Helene

A well-known cold dessert from France.

3 ripe pears
1/2 cup water
2 Tbsps. rice syrup
1/2 cup nougat cream (see recipe)
***Tofu* ice cream (see recipe)**

Peel the pears, halve them, and remove the seeds. Bring some water and rice syrup to a boil, add the pears, and simmer for 15 minutes. Let the pear concoction cool. Put some *tofu* ice cream in a glass bowl, top with one pear half, and cover with warm nougat cream.

Happy Hedgehogs

This dessert is ideal for children's parties.

4 steamed pear halves
3 oz. almond sticks
1/2 cup raisins
4 Tbsps. carob powder
1 Tbsp. apple-pear concentrate
4 Tbsps. hazelnut butter

Mix the carob powder, apple-pear concentrate, hazelnut butter, and enough water to make a cream. Cover the pear halves with the cream, leaving the small end of the pear exposed (this is the hedgehog's head). Place two raisins on the exposed pear for the hedgehog's eyes. Stand the almond sticks in the cream for the hedgehog's thick hair. —See page 52.

Carob-Fruit

First, prepare a carob cream (see recipe). Add a variety of fruits, such as strawberries, grapes, or pear pieces, to the cream. Skewer each piece of fruit with a party stick, arrange on a plate, and serve.

Millet Souffle

A delicious warm dessert for the winter season.

3 cups millet
6 cups water
Touch of sea salt
4 Tbsps. raisins
Natural vanilla
Cinnamon
Grated lemon rind
4 Tbsps. rice syrup
2 lb. apples

Wash the millet and cook in water with salt, raisins, and lemon rind. Meanwhile, peel and core the apples and cut into thin slices. Mix the apples with the rice syrup, cinnamon, and natural vanilla. Put one half of the cooked millet in a pudding form. Add the apple mixture on top, then cover with the rest of the millet.

Bake at 250°C. (480°F.) for 40 minutes.

Bavarian Elderberry Pancake

A very simple dessert made with fragrant elderberry blossoms.

1/2 lb. whole wheat flour
1/2 cup soymilk
Touch of sea salt
3 Tbsps. *mirin*

Work the ingredients into a thick, liquidy pancake batter. Dip elderberry blossoms into the batter (use the stems to hold the blossoms, keeping them free of batter). Deep-fry in hot oil until golden yellow.
Sprinkle immediately with cinnamon and serve.

Milky Rice

1 cup brown rice
2 cups soymilk
2 Tbsps. rice syrup
1 cinnamon stick
2 cloves
Grated lemon rind
Touch of sea salt

Wash the rice and cook soft with the other ingredients. Remove the cinnamon stick and serve the rice in bowls, sprinkled with cinnamon on top.

Steamed Dumplings

Also called "germ dumplings," we choose to make them with sourdough instead of yeast.

Prepare a dough following the *Sourdough* recipe. Divide the dough into big pieces, fill each with plum compote, and form into dumplings. Let rise for 30 minutes. Boil in salt water and cover with melted margarine. Cover with liquid poppy seed filling (as in the *Poppy Seed Strudel* recipe).

Viennese Jam-Filled Dumplings

For this recipe, prepare a sourdough. Roll out the dough and cut into 3¼-inch squares. In the middle of each piece, put some plum compote, fold up the corners, and press the edges together. Melt some margarine in a fireproof baking pan, and turn the dumplings over in it. Place the dumplings in the pan so that there is some space between them, since they will puff up while baking. Bake at 230°C. (445°F.) for 40 minutes.

These dumplings are also delicious served with warm vanilla sauce (see recipe). You can also leave the dumplings unfilled.

Fruit Dumplings

You can use apricots, strawberries, or plums for this dumpling recipe.

1 lb. whole wheat flour
Touch of sea salt
1/2 lb. *tofu*
5 Tbsps. rice syrup
1 cup whole meal crumbs
1 lb. fresh fruit

Knead the whole wheat flour with the sea salt, rice syrup, *tofu*, and some lukewarm water. Roll out the dough. Cut out pieces from the dough, and place pitted fruit on them. Then, fold the dough over the fruit to form dumplings.

Steam the dumplings in a bamboo steamer, or boil in water with some sea salt. Roast the whole meal crumbs in vegetable margarine and roll the cooked dumplings in it. Sprinkle with cinnamon and serve.

Plum Compote Pockets

This recipe originates from Hungary. To keep its traditional flavor, plum compote should be used as a filling rather than some other marmalade. The characteristic taste of plum compote makes this a delicacy.

Prepare a strudel dough and roll it out. Cut out round pieces from the dough. Fill the dough pieces with plum compote, and fold the dough over the filling. Boil the pockets in salt water. Roast some whole wheat crumbs in margarine and roll the pockets in them. Serve hot.

Viennese Stuffed Pancakes

1 cup whole wheat flour
Touch of sea salt
2 Tbsps. sunflower oil
Unsweetened apricot marmalade

Prepare a thin pancake dough out of the flour, salt, oil and some water. Make thin pancakes in an oiled skillet. Fill with marmalade and roll up the pancakes.

Tofu Stuffed Pancakes

In Austria, stuffed pancakes are a favorite dish. Here, we use *tofu* as the stuffing.

1 cup whole wheat flour
Touch of sea salt
2 Tbsps. sunflower oil
Water
Filling: 1 lb. *tofu*
Natural vanilla
Grated lemon rind
3 Tbsps. apple-pear concentrate
1 pitted *umeboshi* plum
3 Tbsps. washed raisins

Make a thin, watery dough from the flour, salt, oil, and water, and make the pancakes. Fill with the *tofu* filling (prepared as for the *tofu* strudel). Fold the pancakes in half to cover the *tofu* and serve.

Semolina Schmarren

The word *schmarren* comes from Austria, and refers to a sweet grain dish.

1 qt. soymilk
1 Tbsp. vegetable margarine
2 oz. raisins
1 lb. whole wheat semolina
Touch of sea salt
Natural vanilla

Heat the soymilk with the margarine, raisins, and spices. Stir in the semolina and steam until done. Oil a casserole dish with some margarine, and fill it with the sweet semolina. Bake until the surface is crunchy, then slice into pieces and serve.

Crepes "Surprise"

France invites you to the table.

1 cup whole wheat flour
Touch of sea salt
2 Tbsps. sunflower oil
2 Tbsps. rice syrup

Make a pancake dough out of the ingredients and some water. Oil a skillet and make some very thin crepes out of the dough. Fill the crepes with *tofu* cream (see recipe) and pour some carob cream (see recipe) over them; top with pine nuts.

Sweet Potato Cookies

The sweet potato or yam is unrelated to the common potato.
Although it may have an appearance similar to the potato, it
has a sweet taste and comes originally from Japan.

4 sweet potatoes
1/2 cup raisins
2 Tbsps. rice syrup
3 Tbsps. vegetable margarine
Touch of sea salt or 1 Tbsp. *miso*

Peel the sweet potatoes, steam them for 20 minutes, and mash.
Mix with raisins, rice syrup, and *miso*. Melt the margarine in a
heavy pan. Form small patties from the sweet potato mixture
and pan-fry on each side. Serve either hot or cold.

Emperor's Schmarren

To make this Austrian dish, prepare a pancake dough out of
whole wheat flour, sea salt, and water. Make slightly thick
pancakes in an oiled skillet, and while the pancake is still in the
pan, cut it into smaller pieces. Cover with rice syrup, sprinkle
with cinnamon, and serve.

Baked Apple Wedges

A very simple and quickly prepared dessert.

3 apples
1 cup finely ground whole wheat flour
Touch of sea salt
Cinnamon

Make a thick batter out of the flour, salt, and some water. Wash the apples, then core and cut them into quarters. Dip the apples in the batter and deep-fry them in hot oil. Sprinkle with cinnamon.

Plum Pavesen

6–8 whole grain rolls
5 1/2 oz. plum jam
Cinnamon
1 cup fine whole wheat flour
Touch of sea salt

Prepare a thick batter out of the flour, salt, and some water. Cut the rolls into slices, and put two slices together with plum jam in the middle. Cover these with batter and deep-fry in hot oil. Sprinkle with cinnamon.

Schlosser Buben (Iron Boys)

3 1/2 oz. pitted prunes
1/2 cup peeled almonds
1/2 cup whole wheat flour
Touch of sea salt

Prepare a thick batter out of the whole wheat flour, salt, and some water. Fill the prunes with the almonds. Dip these into the batter and deep-fry in hot sunflower oil. Serve on party sticks.

Baked Apples

Children, come and guess
what is baking in the stove.
How it steams and how it hisses!
We'll soon have ready to eat
with a zipple and a zapple,
the irresistible apple!

4 cooking or baking apples
2 Tbsps. raisins
2 Tbsps. chopped hazelnuts
2 Tbsps. vegetable margarine
4 Tbsps. rice syrup
Cinnamon

Wash the apples. Core them with an apple corer. Fill the center of each apple with a mixture of raisins, nuts, and rice syrup. Top the filling with some margarine, and place the apples in an oiled baking pan. Bake until the skin tears apart slightly. Spinkle with cinnamon and serve.

Porridge With Fruit

Porridge is a mainstay of a traditional English breakfast.

1 cup fine oat flakes
Touch of sea salt
1/4 cup prunes
1/4 cup dried apricots
7 cups water

Bring the water and sea salt to a boil. Stir in the oat flakes. Cut the fruit into small pieces and add to the oats. Cook for 15 minutes while stirring occasionally, then put on a low flame for another 10 minutes. Sprinkle with cinnamon and serve.

Gajar Halva

If you desire something special, prepare this sweet carrot dish from India.

1 1/2 lbs. carrots
1 1/2 qts. soymilk
1 cup rice syrup
1/4 Tbsp. saffron
1/4 Tbsp. cardamon
1 Tbsp. rose water
1 Tbsp. vegetable margarine
1/2 cup grated almonds
1/2 cup split almonds

Wash the carrots and grate finely. Cook the carrots with the soymilk for 2 hours, while stirring occasionally until it thickens. Then add the rice syrup, raisins, and spices. Cook the mixture until it has thickened. Mix in the grated almonds and cook for another 10 minutes. Put the mixture in a shallow, flat, glass baking pan, and decorate with split almonds.

Deep-Fried Melon Wedges

1 1/2 lbs. honeydew melon
4 oz. whole wheat flour
Touch of sea salt
Rice syrup

Slice the melon into wedges and cut off the skin. Prepare a deep-frying batter out of the flour, salt, and some water. Dip the melon wedges into the batter and deep-fry in hot sunflower oil. Dribble some rice syrup on these melon wedges before serving.

Bircher Muesli

In Switzerland, one eats this type of muesli for breakfast. It is named after Dr. Bircher, a nutritional scientist.

3 1/2 oz. fine oat flakes
1 Tbsp. raisins
1 Tbsp. hazelnuts
1 Tbsp. rice syrup
1 cup soymilk
1 apple, finely sliced
1/2 cup strawberries or cherries
Touch of sea salt

Mix all ingredients in a bowl and let sit for 15 minutes. Enjoy!

Black Jewels—Su Chung Kwa

A very exotic, tasty dish from China.

> 1 piece fresh ginger root
> 1 lemon
> 1 cinnamon stick
> 5 black peppercorns
> 1 cup rice syrup
> 1/2 lb. dried persimmons
> 1 Tbsp. chopped pine nuts

Peel the ginger and slice it into thin pieces. Thinly slice the lemon as well. Boil for 20 minutes, together with the cinnamon stick, peppercorns, and 5 cups of water. Strain and add the rice syrup. Marinate the dried persimmons in this mixture overnight.

The next day, strain the juice from the fruit, place the fruit in bowls, and sprinkle with pine nuts to serve.

Note: If you cannot find persimmons, you can use prunes in this dish.

Tubtimkrob

A refreshing delicacy from Thailand.

> 2 cups fresh coconut milk
> 3 Tbsps. rice syrup
> 7 oz. pistachio nuts
> 1 Tbsp. strawberry marmalade
> 1 Tbsp. agar flakes
> Ice cubes

Bring the strawberry marmalade to a boil in 1 cup of water. Stir in the agar flakes and boil for 5 minutes. Let cool slightly. Before this strawberry agar hardens, pour it over the pistachio nuts. Mix the coconut milk with rice syrup, and place in glass bowls with ice cubes. Add the rose-colored pistachios, letting them swim in the sweet coconut milk. Serve.

Fruit Salad

1 peach
1 apple
1 pear
1 Tbsp. chopped walnuts
Lemon juice
2 Tbsps. *mirin*
6 Tbsps. water

Wash the fruit and cut into cubes. Mix all ingredients in a bowl and let sit for 15 minutes. Serve and enjoy.

Cooked Mandarin Oranges

Cook thrice-quartered mandarin oranges for 20 minutes in ½ cup of water and ½ cup of *mirin*. Mix in some rice syrup as sweetener. Serve in small bowls, sprinkling the mandarin oranges with chopped walnuts.

Paludeh With Melon

This fruit salad is a delicacy that comes from Persia.

1 medium-sized honeydew melon
2 peaches
5 Tbsps. rice syrup
2 Tbsps. lemon juice
2 Tbsps. rose water
1 cup shaved ice

Cut the melon in half and remove the seeds. Cut out round melon balls with a round spoon or melon baller. Save the juice. Pour hot water over the peaches, peel them, and cut into thin slices. Mix together the melon, peaches, lemon juice, and rice syrup, and put in the refrigerator.

Mix with the rose water $\frac{1}{2}$ hour before serving. Place in glass bowls, and serve sprinkled with finely shaved ice.

Fruit Compote

You can use any kind of fruit for this dish, such as apples, pears, peaches, apricots, cherries, plums, and so on.

Wash one kind of fruit, quarter or cut it into cubes, and bring to a boil. Use twice as much water as you have fruit. Cook with a piece of lemon rind and a cinnamon stick. Sweeten with some rice syrup. Serve warm or cold.

Puff-Pastry Grapes

Prepare puff pastry dough and roll it out in a thin layer less than $\frac{1}{4}$-inch thick. Cut out rhombus-shaped pieces of dough and deep-fry in hot oil until golden yellow. Let drip on paper towels.

4. Puddings, Creams, and Marmalades

Chestnut Pudding

This pudding has a natural sweetness from the chestnuts. You can additionally sweeten as much as you like with rice syrup.

1 cup chestnut purée
Touch of sea salt
1/2 pack agar flakes

To make chestnut purée, boil chestnuts, peel (be sure to remove the inner skin as well), and mash.

Bring 2 cups of water to a boil, stir in the agar flakes, add the sea salt and the chestnut purée, and after well-mixed, let simmer for 5 minutes. Wet the inside of a baking form to help prevent sticking, and add the chestnut mixture. Cool, then flip over and cut into rectangles to serve.

Plum Pudding

In England, this pudding is served at Christmas time.

4 cups cooked buckwheat
1 cup raisins
1/2 cup chopped prunes
1/2 cup chopped dried apricots

1 cup grated almonds
4 cups whole wheat flour
2 Tbsps. *miso*
5 Tbsps. rice syrup
Grated orange and lemon rind
Cinnamon
Clove powder
Natural vanilla

Mix all ingredients well, and place in a fireproof baking dish. Steam in a water bath for 1½ hours. Serve warm. —See page 49.

Tapioca Pudding

A delicacy from Malaysia for hot summer days.

2 Tbsps. sago
2 Tbsps. rice syrup
1 cup soymilk
Touch of sea salt
3 Tbsps. coconut flakes
Natural vanilla

Heat the soymilk with 1 cup of water, sea salt, rice syrup, natural vanilla, and coconut flakes. Add the sago while constantly stirring, then simmer over a low flame for 15 minutes until the sago is transparent. Serve with fresh fruit.

Pumpkin Custard

This dessert comes from the United States, and is a good wintertime treat.

2 lbs. Hokkaido pumpkin
2 cups soymilk
1 cup mashed *tofu*
1 Tbsp. cornstarch
Touch of sea salt
Cinnamon
Nutmeg
Gingerbread spices
Ginger powder

Cut the Hokkaido pumpkin into big pieces and cook until soft on a low flame. Purée in a food mill or press through a strainer. Add the soymilk and mashed *tofu* to the pumpkin purée. Add all the other ingredients except the nutmeg. Put into an oiled baking pan and grate the nutmeg over the pumpkin mixture. Let it harden in a warm oven. Serve cold.

Semolina Flammeri Pudding

This light grain pudding is suitable as a filling between-meals snack.

1/2 qt. soymilk
1/2 cup whole wheat semolina
1 cup mashed *tofu*
3 Tbsps. rice syrup
1/2 cup *amazake*
1/2 cup raisins
1/2 cup grated almonds
Touch of sea salt
Grated lemon rind

Combine the soymilk, salt, lemon rind, almonds, rice syrup, *amazake*, raisins, and *tofu* and bring to a boil. Stir in the semolina, then simmer for 10 minutes. Pour into a cold, moist (to help prevent sticking) pudding form. After the pudding has cooled, turn it over.

Pour a bit of *mirin* over the top before serving.

Amandine Di Venezia

An almond dessert that comes from Venice.

2 oz. peeled almonds
1 cup mashed *tofu*
1/2 cup almond butter
4 Tbsps. rice syrup
Touch of sea salt
3 Tbsps. cornstarch

Boil the almond butter in 2 cups of water, along with the salt and rice syrup. Mix the cornstarch with some cold water, and stir into the boiling mixture. Let simmer for 5 minutes. Mix in the mashed *tofu*. Chop the almonds and dry-roast them. Then, mix them in as well. Put into bowls to cool and serve.

Vermicelles

This dish is also known as "chestnut rice" or vermicelli. In Switzerland, it is found on virtually every menu.

14 oz. chestnuts
1/2 qt. water
4 Tbsps. rice syrup
Juice of 1 orange
Grated orange rind
Natural vanilla

Boil the chestnuts until soft. Peel the chestnuts and purée in a mixer, adding the natural vanilla, orange juice, and rice syrup. The mixture should be firm so that it can be formed into a ball. Grate the chestnut mixture, so that you form small pieces like grains of rice. Garnish with orange rind.

Almond Jelly

This dessert comes from Japan, and does not taste sweet, which is common among desserts from Japan.

**10 Tbsps. *kinako*
3 Tbsps. sunflower oil
5 Tbsps. *kuzu*
1/2 Tbsp. sea salt
2 1/2 cups water
3 Tbsps. grated almonds**

Mix the *kinako* and oil together, add the water, salt, and almonds, and then stir until smooth with a whisk. Bring to a boil, dissolve the *kuzu* in some cold water, and stir into the mixture. Cook for 10 minutes until the mixture thickens. Put into a moist baking pan, let cool, then turn over. Cut into rectangular pieces, sprinkle with black sesame seeds, and serve.

Carob Cream

This cream recalls a conventional nougat cream, and can be used as one.

**1 cup carob powder
2 Tbsps. vegetable margarine
3 Tbsps. apple-pear concentrate
5 Tbsps. hazelnut butter**

Heat the margarine and the hazelnut butter. Slowly stir in the apple-pear concentrate and the carob powder. Cook for 5 minutes. If you desire a thinner, more liquidy cream, use more margarine.

Kinako Cream

This cream is prepared in the same manner as the carob cream (above), but instead of carob, use *kinako* (roasted soy flour), and instead of hazelnut butter, use almond butter. This results in a light cream that can be used for cake frosting or for torte fillings.

Halvah

Named after a Greek specialty, Halvah reminds one of a nougat made of honey and sesame.

3/4 lb. whole wheat semolina
7 oz. barley malt
3 cups soymilk
2 cups water
4 Tbsps. olive oil

Roast the semolina in the oil in a hot pan until light brown. Add the soymilk, water, and barley malt. Bring to a boil and stir until the semolina thickens. Place in a moist baking pan, and cut into small cubes when it has cooled. Sprinkle with sesame seeds.

Carob Pudding

1/2 qt. soymilk
1/2 cup carob powder
4 Tbsps. cornstarch

**2 Tbsps. hazelnut butter
2 Tbsps. rice syrup
Touch of sea salt**

Heat the soymilk with the rice syrup, sea salt, and nut butter. Dilute the cornstarch and carob in cold water and stir into the soymilk. Simmer for ten minutes and fill into moistened pudding forms. After it has cooled, turn over and remove the forms.

Tofu Whipped Cream

**1/2 lb. *tofu*
2 Tbsps. rice syrup
6 Tbsps. sunflower oil
Touch of sea salt
Natural vanilla
1/2 cup soymilk**

Mix all ingredients in a blender until smooth. Refrigerate for a few minutes and serve immediately. Tastes great as a topping on pies and tortes.

Tofu-Fruit Cream

**1/2 lb. fresh strawberries
3/4 lb. *tofu*
2 Tbsps. rice syrup
Finely chopped nuts for garnish**

Mix the ingredients (except the nuts) in a blender and fill into bowls. Decorate each bowl with the nuts and one whole strawberry. —See page 51.

Tofu Ice Cream

This ice cream is not as creamy as milk-based ice cream, but it is just as refreshing. You can change the flavor by using fresh strawberries, instant grain coffee, or hazelnut butter.

1 lb. *tofu*
4 Tbsps. barley malt
1/4 tsp. natural vanilla
Touch of sea salt
1 Tbsp. nut oil
1 bowl agar jelly (very hard and diced)

Prepare the agar jelly the day before and keep it in the refrigerator. To prepare the agar jelly, boil ½ pack of agar flakes in ½ quart of water, then let it cool.

Mix all ingredients in a blender and place in the freezer for 1 hour. Mix with a whisk, then place overnight in the freezer. Cut into small pieces and mix. Mix again with 3½ ounces of chilled *tofu*. Serve immediately.

Nut Kanten

1/2 qt. water
1/2 qt. soymilk
Touch of sea salt
1/2 jar hazelnut butter
5 Tbsps. rice syrup
Natural vanilla
1/2 pack agar flakes

Boil all the ingredients for 5 minutes while stirring constantly. Put into a baking pan and turn over after it has solidified and cooled. The *kanten* stays liquidy for a while, but hardens in time, perhaps 1 hour, into a gelatin. —See page 54.

Pumpkin Kanten

This dessert is often served during a traditional tea ceremony in Japan.

1 Hokkaido pumpkin
1 cup raisins
5 Tbsps. rice syrup
1 pack agar flakes
Natural vanilla
Juice of 1 lemon

Wash the pumpkin and halve it. Remove the seeds and cut into small pieces. Boil until soft in salt water, then add the raisins and mix in a blender. Bring the purée to a boil, and add the rice syrup, natural vanilla, and the lemon juice. Stir in the agar flakes and let simmer for 5 minutes. Pour into a large, flat baking pan, and let cool. Once it has jelled, cut into rectangular pieces. —See page 52.

Vanilla Sauce

This sauce can be eaten warm or cold and served with many dishes, such as apple strudel or Viennese jam-filled dumplings.

1/2 qt. soymilk
6 Tbsps. almond butter
5 Tbsps. rice syrup
Natural vanilla
Grated lemon rind
3 Tbsps. arrowroot

Heat the soymilk with all the ingredients except the arrowroot. Dilute the arrowroot in some cold water and stir into the soymilk mixture.

Fruit Jelly

Fruit jellies are very popular in Japan, and are eaten during many festivals.

**1/2 pack agar flakes
1 cup fresh strawberries
4 Tbsps. rice syrup
Juice of 2 lemons
Touch of sea salt
1 qt. water**

Clean and halve the strawberries. Bring to a boil the water, rice syrup, and lemon juice. Stir in the agar flakes, quickly bring to a boil, then add the halved strawberries and boil for 15 min-utes more. Pour into a moistened baking pan and let cool and harden. Cut into cubes to serve.

As an alternative, pour into several small bowls, then turn over after the mixture has cooled and jelled. —See page 52.

Red Groats

A very popular German dessert, this dish is often served with hot vanilla sauce.

**1/2 lb. fresh raspberries
3/4 lb. fresh red currants
5 Tbsps. rice syrup
5 Tbsps. cornstarch**

Wash the fruits and mix with some water in a blender. Boil the mixed fruits with the rice syrup and a touch of sea salt. Dilute the cornstarch in some cold water, then stir into the fruit mixture. Bring to a boil, then pour into a cold, moistened baking pan, and let cool.

Apricot Cream

This is a refreshing cream with a savory taste.

5 1/2 Tbsps. dried apricots
1 Tbsp. almond butter
1/4 qt. soymilk
1/4 Tbsp. nutmeg
1/4 qt. water
Juice from 2 oranges

Soak the apricots overnight in the orange juice. Mix in a blender, slowly adding the soymilk. Add the remaining ingredients. You can vary the thickness of the cream by changing the amount of soymilk you use.

Apple Butter

2 1/4 lbs. apples
Touch of sea salt

Halve the apples, then core and cut them into quarters. Cook the apple quarters until soft with some sea salt and just enough water to cover. Mix in a blender.

Powidl

This powidl should not be confused with plum butter. It is cooked for a long time, resulting in a sweeter and somewhat smoky taste.

4 1/2 lbs. plums
Touch of sea salt

Pit the plums. Add the sea salt and boil on a low flame until very dark and thick. This can take up to 2 hours. Stir often.

Sunrise

You can use homemade fruit juice or fresh fruit in this recipe.

1/2 qt. currant juice
1 cup rice syrup
2 1/2 oz. whole wheat semolina
Natural vanilla
Touch of sea salt

Bring the juice, rice syrup, vanilla, and sea salt to a boil. Stir in the semolina and simmer for 10 minutes. Pour into a bowl and beat with a whisk until foamy. Serve in bowls.

"Noisette" Rice Cream

If you have left-over rice, try this recipe.

2 cups rice soup
2 Tbsps. rice syrup
Juice of 1 lemon
1 peeled and cored apple
4 Tbsps. hazelnut butter

The rice soup is made by cooking 1 cup of cooked brown rice with 7 cups of water overnight on a very low flame.

Mix all ingredients in a blender. Boil for a short time and serve warm.

Pear Butter

4 1/2 lbs. pears
1/2 cup lemon juice
1 cup rice syrup
2 Tbsps. cinnamon
3 Tbsps. grated cloves
1/2 Tbsp. nutmeg

Core the pears and cut into pieces. Bring to a boil along with the remaining ingredients, until all the liquid is gone. Cook for an additional 2½ hours on a low flame until it becomes a thick mixture. Allow to cool, then fill in a jar.

Mirin Fruit

This fruit is prepared in a manner similar to the original rum pot. However, because of the low alcohol content of *mirin*, this dessert will not keep as long as traditional rum-soaked fruits. The length of time that the fruit keeps will vary, between 8 to 14 days.

Fresh fruit such as strawberries, cherries, raspberries, blackberries, and so on can be used. Put the fruit in a bowl and pour some rice syrup over it. Let sit for 2 hours.

Now, put the fruit mixture into a stoneware pot or a jar and fill with *mirin*. The *mirin* should cover the fruit so that it is about ½ inch above the top of the fruit. Cover with cellophane and let sit for 2 days in a cool place. Eat as soon as possible.

Marmalade

2 lbs. fresh fruit in season
1 cup *kuzu*
Touch of sea salt

Wash and cut up the fruit, removing the seeds. Add the salt, and cook the fruit until soft. Dilute the *kuzu* in some cold water and add to the fruit. Cook for about 5 minutes until it thickens. Keep in jars until you use the marmalade.

5. Homemade Candies & Sweet Drinks

Spoil yourself and your loved ones with homemade confectionary. The following recipes are easily and quickly made.

Carob Truffles

1 1/2 Tbsps. vegetable margarine
3 1/2 oz. carob powder
1 cup rice syrup
3 Tbsps. *mirin*
1 Tbsp. hazelnut butter
1 Tbsp. instant grain coffee

Beat the margarine until foamy. Slowly add the rice syrup, then the carob powder, hazelnut butter, grain coffee, and *mirin.* Form into small balls and roll in carob powder. —See page 53.

Kinako Candies

1 cup *kinako*
1/2 cup rice syrup
2 Tbsps. water

Boil ¼ of the *kinako* with the rice syrup and water on a low flame for about 7 minutes. Stir constantly until it thickens. Pour this syrup over the remaining *kinako* and mix thoroughly. Knead into a firm dough; if necessary, add more *kinako.* Shape this dough into a 1-inch-thick roll. Now, cut the roll into ¾-inch-long pieces. Place in the refrigerator overnight; letting them sit improves their taste.

Marzipan

1 lb. small white beans
1/2 lb. grated almonds
1 cup barley malt
Natural vanilla
3 Tbsps. *mirin*
4 Tbsps. almond butter

Soak the beans overnight, then cook until soft and mash. Mix with the remaining ingredients to form a firm mixture. Form into a large ball and place in the refrigerator overnight.

If you add chopped parsley, you can make green marzipan and can shape pieces into small leaves. With both green and white marzipan, you can make beautiful flowers.

Stuffed Dates

20 dried, pitted dates
3 oz. marzipan (see recipe above)
1 oz. finely chopped pistachios

Mix the marzipan with the pistachios and form into small balls. Put these balls into the pitted dates. Make several little notches into the exposed marzipan. —See page 56.

Easter Eggs

Prepare a chestnut purée as in the *Vermicelles* recipe. Form small balls from the purée and cover with carob cream (see recipe for carob cream). Put into small paper forms and use to decorate the table during Easter.

Prassad

This is an East Indian sweet. It is a food that is offered to temple visitors as a holy gift, in a manner similar to communion in the West.

> 1/2 lb. corn semolina
> 1/2 qt. water
> 2 oz. sunflower oil
> 2 oz. raisins
> 2 oz. chopped almonds
> 2 oz. marzipan (see recipe)
> 1 1/2 oz. barley or rice syrup
> 2 oz. dates
> 1 oz. grated coconut

Chop the marzipan and dates. Toast the corn semolina in oil while constantly stirring. Add the water slowly, then boil on a low flame for 20 minutes until the mixture firms. Take the pot from the stove and add the remaining ingredients. Mix everything together well and let cool. Form into small balls and roll in the grated coconut.

Plum Confectionery

> 8 oz. pitted prunes
> 3 oz. grated hazelnuts
> 2 oz. apricot marmalade
> 4 oz. fine oat flakes
> Lemon juice
> Carob powder

Wash the prunes and chop them into small pieces. Mix with the remaining ingredients and press this mixture between two boards; place a weight on the top board for more pressure. After 1 to 2 days, cut into cubes and roll in carob powder.

Marzipan Potatoes

Prepare some marzipan (see recipe). Form it into small balls, roll in carob powder, then score one side of the balls so that they look like boiled potatoes in their skins.

Fig Dumplings

1/2 lb. marzipan (see recipe)
8 dried figs
4 Tbsps. apricot marmalade
3 1/2 oz. grated hazelnuts

Cut the figs into quarters. Cover each fig piece with marzipan and form into small balls. Heat the apricot marmalade and stir it until smooth. Roll the balls in the marmalade, and afterward, roll them in the hazelnuts to form fig dumplings.

Candied Almonds

1 cup peeled almonds
3 Tbsps. barley malt

Heat the barley malt with 2 tablespoons of water. Put the almonds in a bowl and mix the barley malt into them. Spread the almonds on a baking pan and let them harden.

Sesame Taffy

1/2 lb. white sesame seeds
5 Tbsps. barley malt

Put the sesame seeds in a bowl. Heat the barley malt and mix it in with the sesame seeds. The barley malt should just cover the sesame seeds. Put the mixture onto a baking tin. After it has cooled, cut into rectangular pieces. —See page 55.

Candied Popcorn

This happy dish comes from the United States.

2 Tbsps. popcorn
1 1/2 Tbsps. oil
4 Tbsps. maple syrup

Heat the oil in a wide pot. then add the popcorn. Shake the pot continuously while the corn is popping to avoid burning. After popping the corn, pour the maple syrup over it and mix it up well.

Sweet Nut Mix

1/2 cup cashew nuts
1/2 cup walnuts
1/2 cup pine nuts
Rice syrup

Toast the nuts in a pan, and while they are still hot, pour the rice syrup over them so that they are well-coated.

Salty Nut Mix

1/2 cup white sesame seeds
1/2 cup dried pumpkin seeds
1/2 cup sunflower seeds
Shoyu (naturally processed soy sauce,
often called *tamari* soy sauce in
macrobiotic cookbooks)

Roast each type of seed separately until they are light brown. Immediately after roasting, sprinkle with *shoyu*. Mix the *shoyu*-roasted seeds together.

Ice On A Stick

For the little ones (and for adults as well), this dessert is a refreshing welcome in the summertime.

Mix any fresh fruit together with some rice syrup into a mash, and fill one or several ice forms with this mixture. (You can buy such forms in most hardware or kitchenware stores). Put these in the freezer for 24 hours.

As a change, you can also mix some soymilk in with the fruit.

Fruit Bowl

The perfect refreshment for a summer party.

1 qt. natural apple juice or cider
1 qt. mineral water
Fresh fruits of your choice
2 Tbsps. rice syrup
3 Tbsps. *mirin*

Cut the fruit into small pieces, and put them with the remaining ingredients in a large punch bowl. Leave in the refrigerator overnight.

Woodruff Bowl

An aromatic drink, also known as a "May bowl."

1 qt. natural apple juice
1 bundle fresh woodruff (mayweed) leaves
1 qt. mineral water
Juice of 1 lemon
3 Tbsps. *mirin*
2 Tbsps. rice syrup

Soak the woodruff leaves for 3 hours in the apple juice. Take them out and add the remaining ingredients to the apple juice. Do not use the woodruff leaves again.

Bancha Punch

2 cups *bancha* tea
Cloves
1 cinnamon stick
Lemon rind
2 Tbsps. rice syrup
Juice of 1 orange

Boil the *bancha* tea with the rest of the ingredients for 10 minutes, then strain the solids.

Kokoh Drink

Kokoh, also called "grain milk," is a tasty mixture of grains and seeds. It is delicious as a porridge or can be used in baking. Following is a recipe for a drink made from *kokoh*.

2 Tbsps. *kokoh*
Touch of sea salt
2 Tbsps. rice syrup

Add the *kokoh* to 1 quart of water and bring to a boil. Simmer for 20 minutes while constantly stirring. Sweeten with the rice syrup.

You can buy *kokoh*, or you can make it yourself:

1 cup brown rice flour
1/2 cup sweet brown rice flour
1/2 cup oat flour
2 Tbsps. ground sesame seeds
2 Tbsps. ground *azuki* beans

Toast the flours separately in a pan. After toasting, mix together.

Note: For people with digestive problems or for young children, it is better to make the *kokoh* from cooked whole grains rather than flour. The cooked grains can be mashed or put through a hand mill. *Kokoh* is *not* a substitute for breast milk, and should *not* be used as an infant's sole weaning food.

Strawberry Shake

2 cups soymilk
1 bowl fresh strawberries
2 Tbsps. rice syrup

Mix all ingredients and pour into glasses.
This and all other soymilk drinks should be used mainly in the summer, as soymilk has a strong cooling effect.

Almond Milk

2 cups soymilk
2 Tbsps. almond butter
2 Tbsps. rice syrup

Mix all ingredients and fill into glasses.

Carob Mocha Shake

2 cups soymilk
2 Tbsps. carob powder
1 Tbsp. grain coffee
2 Tbsps. rice syrup

Mix all ingredients together, pour into glasses, and sprinkle with carob.

Viennese Ice Coffee

4 Tbsps. grain coffee
2 cups water
3 Tbsps. rice syrup
***Tofu* ice cream (see recipe)**

Dilute the grain coffee in the cold water and sweeten with rice syrup. Put in glasses and add small scoops of the *tofu* ice cream. Top with some *tofu* cream (see recipe).

Amazake

Amazake is a sweet drink made from fermented rice. It can be store-bought, or you can easily make it yourself. *Amazake* is also an excellent sweetener for creams and puddings. Tortes can be made lighter by using *amazake*.

1 cup sweet brown rice
2 cups water
1/4 cup *koji*

Pressure-cook the sweet brown rice with the water for 45 minutes. Let cool for ten minutes, then add the *koji*. Warm the oven to its lowest setting and let the rice mixture sit in it for 8 to 12 hours. Mix thoroughly in a blender. If you wish to prepare *amazake* as a drink or cream, you can thin it with water to the desired consistency.

Rice Soup Drink

2 bowls rice soup (it is OK if it is slightly sour)
3 Tbsps. rice syrup
Juice of 1 lemon

Rice is a nutritious breakfast food, and takes little time to make in the morning, with some preparation the night before. In the evening, boil 2 parts brown rice with 14 parts water and a touch of sea salt for 40 minutes. Turn off the flame and let the rice sit overnight. In the morning, boil the rice soup another 10 minutes while stirring constantly. This is a delicious, creamy dish.

Mix the rice soup with the rice syrup and lemon juice in a blender. This makes a refreshing, somewhat sweet and sour drink.

Maple Candies

1 cup maple syrup
1/2 cup soymilk
1 1/2 Tbsps. sunflower oil
1 Tbsp. natural vanilla
2 oz. grated almonds
2 oz. split almonds

Mix the maple syrup and soymilk, and boil for 5 minutes. Add to the remaining ingredients, and form small balls. If the mixture is still too soft to form balls, add more nuts. After these balls sit for one day, they harden into candies. —See page 50.

Elderberry Juice

1 1/2 qts. water
1 lb. elderberries
Touch of sea salt

October is the season for elderberries. Remove the stems from the elderberries, and boil with water and salt for about 30 minutes. Strain this juice to remove the seeds. Sweeten to taste with rice syrup.

Ice Tea

Boil one bag of *Mu* tea for 10 minutes in 2 cups of water. Let cool, then mix with 2 cups apple juice and the juice of 1 orange.

Oat Milk

3 Tbsps. oat flakes
Touch of sea salt
2 Tbsps. rice syrup
2 cups water

Dry-roast the oat flakes, pour in the boiling water, and season with rice syrup and sea salt. Boil for 5 to 10 minutes. Mix in a blender.

Apricot Slices

1/2 lb. dried apricots
Juice of 1 lemon
1/2 lb. grated coconut

Briefly boil the apricots with a little water, then let sit for 3 hours. Pour off the water, mix the apricots with the grated coconut, and add the lemon juice. Knead the mixture to form a dough. If the mixture is too thin, add some more coconut. Form into a loaf, then cut into ¼-inch slices. Roll the slices in coconut if you wish.

Aranzini

The Italian name for this dish comes from *arancia*, which means oranges.

1 Tbsp. rice syrup
Touch of sea salt
1 Tbsp. agar flakes
Grated coconut
2 oranges

Peel the oranges and cut the rind into ¼-inch-wide strips. Boil the rinds in slightly salted water for 15 minutes, then discard the water. Repeat once.

Combine the rice syrup, agar flakes, and ½ cup of water, and bring to a boil. Add the boiled orange rind. Drain any excess, let dry, and roll in the coconut.

Soy Buttermilk

3 cups hot soymilk
2 Tbsps. rice syrup
1 1/2 Tbsps. lemon juice

Mix the soymilk and rice syrup in the blender. Slowly add the lemon juice, while stirring constantly. Let the mixture sit for 1 minute, then mix one more time. Serve immediately.

Glossary

Azuki Beans Small red beans, originally from the Orient.

Agar A jelling agent, made from sea vegetables. Also called kanten.

Amazake A sweet mash made from fermented rice.

Arrowroot A starch made from arrowroot, usually available as a flour. It is used as a thickener for soups, sauces, and creams.

Bancha Roasted tea, usually made from the twigs rather than the leaves of the tea bush. The highest quality bancha is aged for several years.

Barley Malt A sweetener made from sprouted barley grains.

Carob Usually bought as a fine powder, is made from the fruit of the carob tree. It has a taste similar to cacao, from which chocolate comes.

Kinako Roasted flour made from soybeans.

Koji Grains of rice that have been impregnated with mold. When added to starches, the mold sweetens the food by breaking down the starch into simpler sugars.

Kokoh A mixture of grains and seeds, it is good for the preparation of grain milk.

Kuzu A high-quality thickening agent made from kuzu root.

Maple Syrup   The sap of maple trees that is boiled down to become a sweet syrup.

Mirin   Sweet brown rice vinegar, about 14% alcohol.

Miso   A salty paste made from fermented soybeans and grains. The highest quality misos have been aged for several months or years.

Mochi   A cake made of pounded, cooked sweet rice.

Mu Tea   A medicinal tea made with various herbs.

Rice Syrup   A sweetener made from sprouted rice grains.

Sago   Starch flour that can be used as a thickener, made from the tapioca (cassava, manioc) plant.

Shoyu   Also known as soy sauce, a salty liquid seasoning made from fermented soybeans and grains.

Tofu   A curd (cheese) made from soybeans.

Recipe Index